Eleanor Roosevelt

Publishing Company

by
Sarah Tieck

VISIT US AT
www.abdopublishing.com

Published by ABDO Publishing Company, 8000 West 78th Street, Edina, Minnesota 55439.

Copyright © 2010 by Abdo Consulting Group, Inc. International copyrights reserved in all countries. No part of this book may be reproduced in any form without written permission from the publisher. Buddy Books™ is a trademark and logo of ABDO Publishing Company.

Printed in the United States of America, North Mankato, Minnesota
092009
012010

♻ PRINTED ON RECYCLED PAPER

Coordinating Series Editor: Rochelle Baltzer
Contributing Editors: Heidi M.D. Elston, Megan M. Gunderson, BreAnn Rumsch, Marcia Zappa
Graphic Design: Jane Halbert
Cover Photograph: *AP Photo*: AP Photo
Interior Photographs/Illustrations: *AP Photo*: AP Photo (pp. 5, 7, 9, 10, 12, 13, 14, 15, 17, 19, 21, 23, 29), Keystone (p. 6), Donald Stampfli (p. 27), Stf (p. 24); *Getty Images*: Stock Montage (p. 19).

Library of Congress Cataloging-in-Publication Data

Tieck, Sarah, 1976-
  Eleanor Roosevelt / Sarah Tieck.
    p. cm. -- (First biographies)
  ISBN 978-1-60453-986-8
  1. Roosevelt, Eleanor, 1884-1962--Juvenile literature. 2. Presidents' spouses--United States--Biography--Juvenile literature. I. Title.
  E807.1.R48T58 2010
  973.917092--dc22
  [B]
                          2009031073

Table of Contents

Who Is Eleanor Roosevelt? 4

Eleanor's Family 6

School and Work..8

Starting a Family 12

Big Dreams..14

First Lady 16

A World War...20

Helping the World...22

An Important Woman 26

Important Dates 30

Important Words 31

Web Sites 31

Index..32

Who Is Eleanor Roosevelt?

Eleanor Roosevelt is a famous First Lady. Her husband was U.S. president during the **Great Depression** and **World War II**. These were hard times for the United States.

Eleanor spent her life helping others. She worked so all people would be treated fairly. And, she created new opportunities for women.

Eleanor's accomplishments made her one of the greatest American First Ladies.

Eleanor's Family

Anna Eleanor "Eleanor" Roosevelt was born on October 11, 1884. She was born in New York City, New York.

New York City, around 1890

Eleanor's parents were Anna and Elliott Roosevelt. Eleanor had two younger brothers named Elliott and Hall.

When Eleanor was young, her parents died. So, other family members raised Eleanor.

Eleanor (*right*) was close with her father. He died in 1894.

School and Work

The Roosevelts were an important and wealthy family. Eleanor's mother had wanted her daughter to be beautiful and stylish. But, Eleanor was considered plain.

In 1899, Eleanor went away to school. She attended Allenswood Academy near London, England. There, she became more sure of herself. Eleanor wanted to help others and change ideas.

Eleanor considered her time at Allenswood important to her life and work.

SCOTLAND

North Sea

NORTHERN IRELAND

IRELAND

WALES

ENGLAND

London ★

Celtic Sea

FRANCE

Eleanor and Franklin had known each other for many years. They were distant cousins.

In 1902, Eleanor returned to New York. There, she took a job working with some of the city's poorest people.

Soon, Eleanor began dating Franklin Delano Roosevelt. Franklin valued her work. He wanted to help people, too.

Starting a Family

Eleanor's uncle Theodore Roosevelt was U.S. president from 1901 to 1909. He inspired Franklin to work in politics.

On March 17, 1905, Eleanor married Franklin in New York City. Between 1906 and 1916, the couple had six children. Sadly, one of their sons died as a baby.

As a wife and mother, Eleanor managed her household and family.

Big Dreams

Franklin hoped to be president someday. But in 1921, he became **paralyzed**. He wasn't sure he could work in **politics**. Still, Eleanor said she would help him follow his dream.

Franklin (*center*) was almost never seen in his wheelchair. So, many people didn't know his legs were paralyzed.

When people run for office, they meet many voters. They tell them their political ideas and plans.

Eleanor often traveled and gave speeches for Franklin. In 1929, Franklin became New York's governor. And in 1932, he ran for president of the United States. He won!

First Lady

In 1933, Franklin became the thirty-second U.S. president. Eleanor became the First Lady. At that time, a First Lady was not usually active in her husband's presidency. But, Eleanor helped Franklin serve as president.

Franklin struggled to walk. So, he asked Eleanor to be his eyes and ears. She traveled throughout the country and told Franklin what she learned.

Eleanor traveled around the world. She visited places such as Puerto Rico to learn about life there.

When Eleanor became First Lady, the United States was in the **Great Depression**. Many people were very poor and out of work.

Also at this time, not all Americans were treated the same. Women were treated differently than men. And, African Americans were often treated unfairly.

Eleanor worked to make life better for all Americans. Today, First Ladies follow Eleanor's example. They work for special causes that are meaningful to them.

Eleanor held press meetings just for female reporters. This helped more women get jobs as journalists.

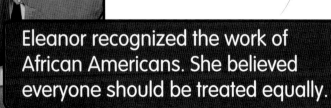

Eleanor recognized the work of African Americans. She believed everyone should be treated equally.

A World War

In 1941, the United States entered **World War II**. Many families were separated as the men left to fight.

This was a difficult time for Americans. They trusted Franklin. In 1944, he was elected president for a fourth time. He began his new term in January 1945. Soon after, Franklin died on April 12.

Deeply saddened, Eleanor left the White House. She had been First Lady for 12 years.

During World War II, Eleanor traveled around the world to meet soldiers. Sometimes, she went to areas where there was fighting.

Helping the World

Eleanor found ways to continue working in **politics** after Franklin's death. In 1945, she started working for the newly formed **United Nations (UN)**. The UN planned to improve life for people throughout the world.

In 1948, Eleanor helped write the UN's **Universal Declaration of Human Rights**. Some say this was her most important accomplishment. Eleanor left the UN in 1952.

Through her work with the UN, Eleanor helped people around the world.

Eleanor gave many speeches after she left the White House. People still wanted to hear her ideas.

In her later years, Eleanor continued to speak out. She wrote about important issues in newspapers and magazines. She also wrote books about her life. And, she spent time with her family.

People remembered what a good First Lady Eleanor had been. She was known for her hard work to help others.

An Important Woman

Around 1961, Eleanor became sick. She died at age 78 on November 7, 1962. She was buried next to Franklin in a rose garden in New York.

After Eleanor's death, people remembered her work. Some wrote books about her life. And in 1968, her life was honored with a **UN** Human Rights Prize.

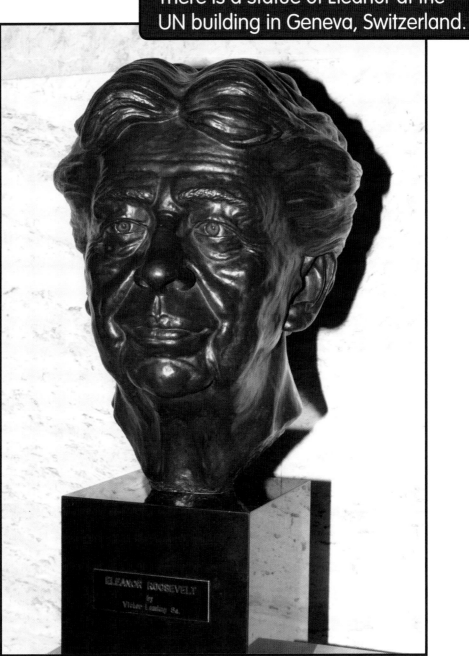

There is a statue of Eleanor at the UN building in Geneva, Switzerland.

ELEANOR ROOSEVELT
by
Victor Lundeng 84.

Today, Eleanor is considered one of the greatest First Ladies in U.S. history. She helped the United States through the **Great Depression** and **World War II**.

During her life, Eleanor made efforts to help people. She supported equal rights for all Americans. She created new opportunities for women. And, she helped protect the rights of people around the world.

Eleanor's work as First Lady set an example for later First Ladies.

Important Dates

1884 Eleanor Roosevelt is born on October 11.

1899 Eleanor starts attending Allenswood Academy.

1905 Eleanor marries Franklin Delano Roosevelt. Over the years, Eleanor and Franklin would have six children.

1933 Eleanor becomes First Lady when Franklin becomes U.S. president.

1945 Franklin dies. Eleanor begins working with the United Nations.

1948 Eleanor helps write the Universal Declaration of Human Rights.

1962 Eleanor Roosevelt dies on November 7.

Important Words

Great Depression the period from 1929 to 1942 of worldwide economic trouble. There was little buying or selling, and many people could not find work.

paralyzed (PEHR-uh-lized) affected with a loss of feeling or motion in part of the body.

politics the art or science of government.

United Nations (UN) a group of nations formed in 1945. Its goals are peace, human rights, security, and social and economic development.

Universal Declaration of Human Rights a written paper that says all people have a right to be treated fairly and live peacefully.

World War II a war fought in Europe, Asia, and Africa from 1939 to 1945.

Web Sites

To learn more about Eleanor Roosevelt, visit ABDO Publishing Company online. Web sites about Eleanor Roosevelt are featured on our Book Links page. These links are routinely monitored and updated to provide the most current information available.

www.abdopublishing.com

Index

awards **26**

education **8, 9, 30**

England **8, 9**

Great Depression **4, 18, 28**

New York **6, 11, 12, 15, 26**

Puerto Rico **17**

Roosevelt, Anna **7, 8**

Roosevelt, Elliott (brother) **7, 8**

Roosevelt, Elliott (father) **7, 8**

Roosevelt, Franklin Delano **4, 10, 11, 12, 13, 14, 15, 16, 20, 22, 26, 30**

Roosevelt, Hall **7, 8**

Roosevelt, Theodore **12**

Switzerland **27**

United Nations (UN) **22, 23, 26, 27, 30**

Universal Declaration of Human Rights **22, 30**

White House **20, 24**

World War II **4, 20, 21, 28**